Can an Old Dog Learn New Tricks?

And Other Questions about Animals

BUFFY SILVERMAN

ILLUSTRATIONS BY COLIN W. THOMPSON

LERNER PUBLICATIONS COMPANY

Minneapolis

Contents

Perhaps you've heard these common sayings about animals:

You can't teach an old dog new tricks!
If you touch a baby bird, the mother will abandon it!

But are these sayings true? Is there any science behind the stories? Come along with us as we explore these old beliefs and more. Find out whether the stories and sayings you've heard about animals are

FACT OR FICTION!

Is Spider Silk Really Stronger Than Steel?

YES! In fact, it is several times stronger than steel of the same thickness. It's even stronger than Kevlar, a material used to make bulletproof vests.

What makes the silk so strong? Spiders spin their silk out of proteins. These chemicals are made of long chains. The way the chains link together in a spider's silk makes it extremely tough.

Spiders use their silk in many different ways. They drop down from silk lines to escape danger. Females spin sacs of silk to protect their eggs while baby spiders develop inside the eggs. Some spiders hide in silk tunnels waiting for an insect or other tasty meal to arrive. Others make trapdoors of silk and dart out of the trapdoor when an insect goes by. Still other spiders depend on strong silk webs to catch their meals.

Scientists are trying to learn how to put proteins together in the same way that spiders do. If they can make silk in a laboratory, they may be able to figure out how to make all kinds of new materials. Maybe people could make clothing that could never be ripped or wear out. Car manufacturers might be able to create a car fender that could easily be bent back into shape if it were dented. Many other new products could be possible as well.

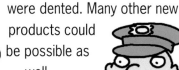

SPIDER VEST

Will a Mother Bird Abandon Her Babies after a Person Touches Them, Because She Smells a Human Scent?

NOPE. Scientists are not even sure that birds can smell people. For years, scientists believed birds had a poor sense of smell because they have tiny olfactory lobes (the part of the brain that detects odors). Modern scientists are not so sure. They are discovering that some birds can smell different odors.

Regardless of whether birds can smell people, they do not abandon their babies after a person has touched them. But birds will not care for their young as long as a person stays near the babies.

If you find a young bird on the ground, you might think it needs your help. Most likely, it does not. A bird with fluffy feathers that is hopping on the ground is a fledgling. It cannot fly well, but it is ready to be out of the nest. Its parents are nearby, ready to feed it and lead it to safety. Leave the fledgling alone, and its parents will return to care for it.

A nestling is a baby bird that isn't ready to be out of the nest. It has few feathers and cannot yet cling to branches. Sometimes nestlings fall out of nests. If you can safely reach a nest, carefully place the nestling back inside. Watch from a distance, so the parents will return.

Fledglings, like this black-throated blue warbler, are young birds that have recently left the nest and are still learning how to fly.

Sniffing Birds

Kiwis are flightless birds that live in New Zealand. They have an excellent sense of smell. A kiwi's olfactory lobe is ten times bigger than that of other birds.

Kiwis are nocturnal (active at night), and they hunt for food in the dark. When a kiwi pushes its beak underground, it sniffs with its nostrils, which are on the tip of its beak. Its sharp sense of smell leads it to worms and bugs.

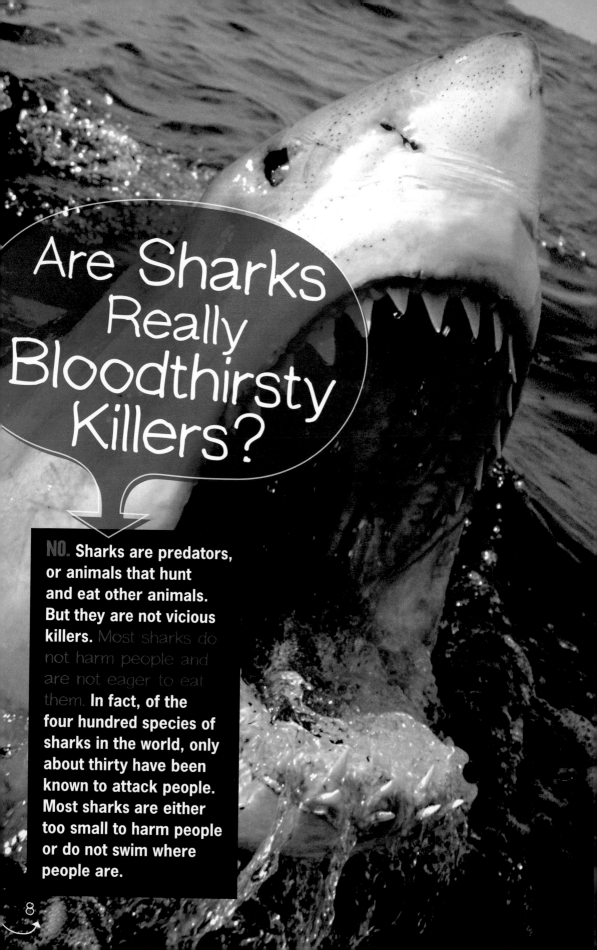

Are Sharks Really Bloodthirsty Killers?

NO. Sharks are predators, or animals that hunt and eat other animals. But they are not vicious killers. Most sharks do not harm people and are not eager to eat them. In fact, of the four hundred species of sharks in the world, only about thirty have been known to attack people. Most sharks are either too small to harm people or do not swim where people are.

The chance of a person being attacked by a shark is very small. Swimmers are much more likely to drown than be injured by sharks. A person in the United States is thirty times more likely to be killed by lightning than by a shark!

Every year, about fifty to seventy-five shark attacks on humans are reported around the world. Many of these attacks occur in shallow water near the shore, where people tend to swim. When sharks hunt for seals, they may grab a swimmer by mistake. Sometimes someone who is fishing gets bitten while catching sharks or trying to free sharks from fishing nets.

Great white sharks hunt for fish and other sea animals—not people.

Three kinds of sharks most often attack people: great white sharks, tiger sharks, and bull sharks. These three shark species sometimes mistake people for their food, since they hunt animals that are about the same size. These sharks usually eat sea turtles, fish, dolphins, seals, and sea lions.

People are much more dangerous to sharks than sharks are to people. Commercial and sport fishers kill about 100 million sharks each year.

This hammerhead shark is caught in a fishing net.

MUNICIPALITY OF ROCKDALE
DANGER
SHARKS IN BOTANY BAY

DOGS ATTRACT SHARKS
PLEASE KEEP
DOGS OUT OF WATER

Can an Old Dog Learn New Tricks?

YES! An older dog takes more time to learn something than a younger dog. But an old dog can definitely learn new tricks. In fact, you can train a pet at any age.

Just like people, dogs have a harder time learning to do new things as they grow older. When a dog (or a person) learns something new, cells in the brain connect to one another. These connections allow the dog—or the person—to remember what was learned. As the dog or person gets older, the brain cells do not make connections as easily. Then learning and remembering become harder.

Scientists have found a way to improve an old dog's memory. They performed an experiment with two groups of elderly beagles. They gave the dogs in one group a special diet with extra nutrients. Nutrients are vitamins and minerals in food. Researchers believe the nutrients keep brain cells healthier. As a result, the cells have more energy and can make new connections.

The researchers tried to teach both groups of dogs how to find a treat behind a colored peg. More of the old dogs on the special diet learned the trick than the old dogs without the special diet. The researchers think that these same nutrients might help older people. They could improve people's memories and their ability to learn new "tricks."

Ostriches cannot fly, but these birds can run fast—up to 43 miles (69 kilometers) per hour! That's probably faster than the speed of your family's car when you drive through a city. With its long, powerful legs, an ostrich outruns many predators. As it runs, it holds its wings out to the side for balance.

If an ostrich cannot run away from danger, it often drops to the ground to try to hide. It lies on the ground with its head and neck stretched flat. Its lightly colored head and neck blend in with the sand. From a distance, it might look as if an ostrich has stuck its head underground. But really, the bird is lying still, hoping that it will not be noticed. If an animal manages to trap the ostrich, the ostrich will try to kick it with its powerful legs. An ostrich kick can injure or kill an attacker.

While ostriches don't bury their heads in sand, they do dip their beaks in it. An ostrich swallows sand and small stones to help it digest its food. Inside its gizzard (a part of its stomach), the sand and stones grind up the hard seeds and insects that the ostrich eats.

An ostrich egg (below) is much larger than the average chicken egg.

Big Eggs

Ostriches are the largest living birds. They can be 10 feet (3 meters) tall. So it's not surprising that they lay the largest eggs. An ostrich egg weighs about as much as two dozen chicken eggs. You'd have to be pretty hungry to eat a scrambled ostrich egg for breakfast!

Is It True That Cats Always Land on Their Feet?

NO, NOT ALWAYS—BUT VERY OFTEN. What makes cats so good at landing upright? It's their skeletons! Cats' skeletons are different from most other animals'. Their backbones can move in many directions. This means that cats can twist and turn while falling, which allows them to land feet first.

A woman examines a cat skeleton. Cats' long backbones are extremely flexible!

Cats in cities fall from windows of tall buildings so often that veterinarians have a name for the problem. They call it high-rise syndrome. Sometimes a cat tries to catch a bird or insect flying past. Then the cat may slip and accidentally fall out the window. By putting screens over windows, people can keep their cats safe.

Researchers at New York's Animal Medical Center studied 132 cats that had fallen out of high-rise windows. Most of the cats survived. The researchers found something surprising. Cats that fell from higher stories were less likely to get hurt than those that fell from lower stories.

Why should cats do better after a higher fall? When a cat begins

to fall, it tenses its legs. If it hits the ground shortly after it falls, its feet and legs are often injured. But if a cat falls farther, it has time to relax and stretch itself out. This position works like a parachute. It slows the cat down. Then, as the cat lands, it arches its back and lands feet first.

Is It True That Bats Are Blind?

NO! The expression "blind as a bat" is not based on scientific fact. All bats can see—although many of them use other senses to help them find food.

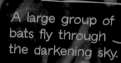

A large group of bats fly through the darkening sky.

Insect-eating bats, for example, use a sense called echolocation to track down their prey. As they fly, these bats make clicking calls with their mouths or noses. They listen for the calls echoing, or bouncing off, a mosquito or a moth. Then they fly toward the echoes until they find the prey.

Fruit-eating bats rely on both their keen noses and their large eyes to find food at night. They smell fruits and nectar from flowers and fly toward them. But if there is no moonlight, fruit bats cannot see well enough to fly, and they go hungry. To find their food, they need to see and smell.

So why do people say that bats are blind when they can see just fine? It may be because bats are nocturnal. Because bats do their hunting when it's dark outside, some people may assume they don't use their eyes at all.

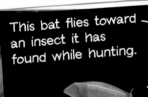

This bat flies toward an insect it has found while hunting.

Did You Know?

Although bats aren't blind, the fleas that live on them are. Bat fleas live in dark places, and these tiny insects can't see at all. So rather than saying, "blind as a bat," maybe we should say, "blind as a bat flea" instead!

Is It True That Porcupines Can Throw Their Quills?

NOPE. Many people believe that porcupines can throw quills the way a person might throw a spear. That's because an animal that attacks a porcupine often gets a mouthful of sharp quills. Porcupines do use their quills to defend themselves. But they can't throw them.

About thirty thousand quills cover a porcupine's body. Each quill has tiny barbs at the end. A barb is like a hook. If a fox, wolf, or other predator attacks, the porcupine becomes frightened. And when a porcupine is frightened, its muscles contract, or tense up. This makes the quills puff up, similar to the way hairs on your arm stand on end if you're cold or frightened. The quills jab into the predator when it tries to make a meal out of the porcupine. When the quills are puffed, they fall off the porcupine easily. But because of those tiny barbs, the quills don't fall off the attacker.

When an animal stuck with porcupine quills moves, its muscles draw the barbs farther into its body. Quills are difficult to pull out. Predators sometimes die from infections caused by the quills. But more often, they learn to avoid the porcupine and its dangerous quills. And a porcupine tries to avoid foxes, wolves, and other predators by climbing a tree when it sees them.

This photo shows a close-up view of the barbs on a porcupine's quill.

Is It True That Fish Don't Sleep?

Every night, you lie down, close your eyes, and become unaware of the world around you. But you never see your goldfish catching any zs! That's because fish don't sleep in the same way we do. **THEY CANNOT LIE DOWN, AND MOST DON'T HAVE EYELIDS TO CLOSE. BUT MOST FISH REST EACH DAY.**

Some fish get most of their sleep in the evening hours—just like you! When night falls, bass and perch rest on or under logs in lakes and rivers. Ocean coral fish rest in crevices of coral reefs, hidden from predators. Fish in an aquarium often move less in the dark.

This fish is resting on some rocks on the bottom of a lake.

Other fish are active at night and rest during the day. Catfish swim around and find food at night. During the day, they rest in hollow logs or in dark, deep pools that they might find below a river dam.

Some fish make beds to shelter them while they rest. Wrasses, which live in shallow ocean waters, burrow into the sand. They use their sharp front teeth to dig a hollow place to rest. Predators do not notice them lying quietly on the ocean floor.

Many sharks probably rest for only a few minutes at a time. That's because they must keep moving to breathe underwater. Oxygen-rich water flows through their gills as they swim. One type of shark—the nurse shark—can stay in one place for a longer period of time. This fish has special openings that force water over its gills even when it isn't swimming. The nurse shark can take longer breaks to rest than other sharks.

These rainbow wrasses have burrowed into the sand to take a rest.

Deep Sleep

In Antarctica, cod survive the harsh winter by hibernating on the seafloor. Their breathing and heartbeat slow down, and their body temperature drops. They use very little energy, so they can survive without eating.

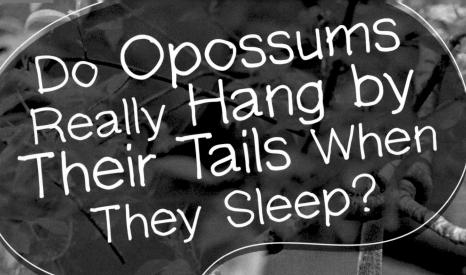

Do Opossums Really Hang by Their Tails When They Sleep?

NOPE. Opossums use their tails for many things, but they don't hang from them while sleeping. Occasionally a young opossum hangs from its tail for a short time while climbing. But an adult opossum is too heavy. Its tail cannot support its weight.

An opossum's tail is prehensile. This means that it can wrap around an object—much like a human's hands. Opossums wrap their tails around tree limbs and branches to balance themselves as they climb. They also use their tails to carry leaves to their nests.

Opossums curl up during the day and sleep in dark, quiet places. Many choose a hollow tree, fallen log, or a brush pile. But some opossums sleep under houses or decks, in garages, and even in attics.

This opossum is curled up in a hollow log to sleep during the day.

Did You Know?

Opossums have no fur on their scaly, pink tails. In cold weather, their tails can get frostbite.

Is It True That the Early Bird Catches the Worm?

FOR BIRDS THAT LOVE WORMS, IT PAYS TO GET UP EARLY. Morning is the perfect time to hunt. Early in the day, you might see a robin hop across a lawn. It turns its head, looking for movement. Suddenly it pushes its beak into the ground and pulls up a worm.

In the afternoon, robins pick berries and find insects. Why don't robins continue to hunt for worms all day long? Earthworms are harder to find when the sun is high.

Earthworms tunnel through damp soil. To breathe through their skin, worms need moisture. In the morning, when dew covers a damp lawn, earthworms crawl close to the surface of the soil.

As the sun rises in the sky, soil near the surface dries. So earthworms travel down deeper, where they are harder for a bird to catch.

Most birds don't catch worms at all. Woodpeckers drill into trees looking for beetles, caterpillars, ants, and other insects. They peck at poison ivy and other plants. Crows love grasshoppers, beetles, spiders, and lizards. They like the eggs of other birds too. Ducks feast on insects in lakes and streams. They also nibble on the seeds and leaves of water plants. Hawks and owls hunt mice, rabbits, fish, and other birds.

Worm Bill

Birds called woodcocks eat worms, just as robins do. A woodcock has the perfect bill for catching worms. It is long and flexible. When hunting worms, the bird pushes its bill into soil and stomps its feet. Worms sense the movement of the bird's feet and crawl away—sometimes right in the direction of the woodcock's bill. The woodcock feels the wriggling worms and snaps its bill shut around its tasty meal.

Can an Alligator Really Live in the Sewer?

NO! People tell stories of alligators roaming New York City's sewers. The underground pipes in these sewers carry away rainwater as well as waste from people's sinks and toilets. But an alligator could never live there.

Some people once claimed that New York City's sewers were filled with gators large enough to eat people who worked in the sewers! According to the tale, in the 1930s, wealthy people brought baby alligators back from Florida. But when the pet alligators grew, they flushed them down the toilet. From there, the alligators traveled down to the sewer system. The alligators caught sewer rats and grew bigger and bigger. Soon colonies of gators roamed underground.

In 1959 the author Robert Daly wrote a book called *The World Beneath the City*. It gave the alligator myth a boost. In the book, he tells about his interview with the New York superintendent of sewers. The superintendent went underground and claimed to see alligator after alligator paddling through the sewers. Other books and movies continued this legend.

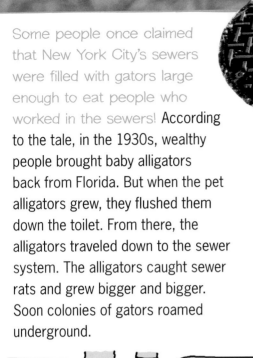

But there's no way that alligators could survive in the icy cold sewers of New York. Alligators do best in warm places, where winters are mild. They prepare for cooler weather by digging tunnels up to 65 feet (20 m) long. When the temperature aboveground gets too cold, they retreat down into their tunnels. Surrounded by soil, they stay warm enough to survive. But in a sewer, there's no place for alligators to escape extreme temperatures.

Another problem with the alligators-in-the-sewer story is that alligators live in swamps, marshes, and other places with plenty of clean, fresh water. They need fresh water to survive. The dirty water in a sewer would soon make an alligator sick.

Do Lemmings Kill Themselves by Jumping Off Cliffs?

NO! Lemmings do sometimes drown when they migrate (move from place to place)—but they do not try to commit suicide.

Did You Know?

Eskimos once believed that lemmings lived in the land beyond the stars and, every few years, lemmings spiraled down to Earth in snowstorms.

Lemmings are rodents that look like small rats. They live in the frozen Arctic tundra. Movies and comic books often show lemmings hurling themselves off cliffs to drown in the sea. People claim that huge numbers of lemmings deliberately kill themselves when they are crowded.

Every four years, lemming populations grow very large. Snowy owls, arctic foxes, wolves, weasels, and other predators hunt lemmings. As the number of lemmings grows, more and more predators are born that eat them. As a result, the lemming population suddenly shrinks. Food shortages and bad weather can also cause the number of lemmings to plunge.

Sometimes when populations of lemmings are very large, they migrate. They travel across the countryside, and even swim across streams and lakes. While lemmings are good swimmers, some drown in windy weather. But they don't jump off tall cliffs.

As a result of this myth, people in a crowd are sometimes compared to lemmings. If someone says that you are acting like a lemming, he or she means that you are not thinking for yourself. Instead, you are doing something foolish by following others.

Is It True That a Worm Can Grow Inside Your Brain?

YES! If the thought of worms crawling through your brain makes you squirm, you are not alone. But for millions of people around the world, worms in the brain are a reality. They cause serious diseases and even death.

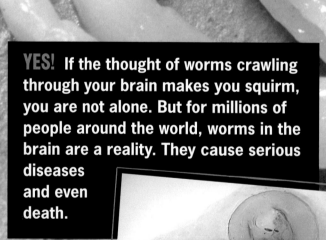

This photo shows a close-up of a pork tapeworm's head.

Worms inside a brain are parasites. Like all parasites, they live on another living being. That living being is called a host. A parasite gets its food by eating the host. Worms inside a brain eat it.

One of the most common worms that can enter a person's brain is the pork tapeworm. People get pork tapeworms from eating pork that isn't cooked well. The tapeworms live in the uncooked pork.

If a person swallows a tapeworm, the worm attaches to the gut, where it can grow several feet long. But sometimes, people eat pork that has tapeworm eggs inside it. The eggs hatch inside a person's stomach. Then they enter the person's bloodstream. From there, they are carried all over the body, and some worms reach the brain.

Most parasites cannot get into a brain. That is because a special layer of cells called the blood-brain barrier protects our brains. These cells are packed tightly around blood vessels going to the brain. The barrier blocks diseases and most parasites from entering the brain. Scientists aren't sure how the pork tapeworm gets through the blood-brain barrier. They think the worm makes chemicals that dissolve the layer of cells so the parasites can sneak through.

Inside the brain, the worms attach to brain tissue. The worms change the way parts of the brain work. They cause headaches, nausea, and dizziness. A person can live for years with a brain tapeworm but may eventually die from it.

The good news is that doctors prescribe drugs that are very good at killing tapeworms. And you can avoid getting tapeworms in the first place by eating only meat that has been cooked properly and by washing your hands before you eat.

Washing your hands before you eat can protect you from getting sick.

Does a Female Praying Mantis Really Eat Her Mate?

SOMETIMES. She may bite off the male's head while they are mating and then devour him.

Praying mantises are large insects that hunt moths, grasshoppers, crickets, and flies. They have an enormous appetite and are even known to eat turtles, mice, frogs, and birds. Newly hatched mantises often eat one another.

A praying mantis is hard to spot because it blends in with grass or other plants where it lives. The mantis waits like a statue for its prey to come near. It can turn its head, searching for movement. When an insect approaches, it strikes with its forelegs.

At the end of the summer, a female praying mantis makes a special chemical called a pheromone. When a male smells this chemical, he approaches. As he nears the female, he may slow down and move cautiously. Maybe he senses that the female can be dangerous. During mating, she may turn and bite off his head. The headless male keeps mating. When the pair is finished, the female devours the rest of the male. Scientists aren't sure how often female mantises eat their mates. They estimate that this happens from 5 to 31 percent of the time. So most males keep their heads!

Female mantises that eat their mates need this extra nourishment. Soon after mating, the female lays her eggs on twigs or on a building. She lays from between twelve and four hundred eggs and surrounds them with a frothy liquid. The liquid hardens, making a tough shell that protects the eggs all winter. It takes a lot of energy for the female to lay her eggs and make the shell. Soon after, the female dies. The eggs hatch the following spring.

Praying mantis eggs in the shell

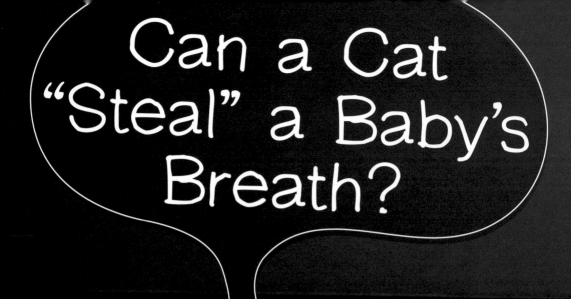

Can a Cat "Steal" a Baby's Breath?

NO! For hundreds of years, people have told stories of cats sucking the breath from a baby. According to the legend, cats were attracted to babies because of the smell of milk on their breath. When a cat found a sleeping baby, it jumped in the baby's crib and sucked air from the baby until it died.

A newspaper article in 1929 quoted a doctor who claimed to have witnessed this act. The doctor said that he found a cat lying on a baby's chest with a paw on each side of the baby's face. The cat's lips were pressed to the baby's mouth, and the cat was sucking. The baby's lips had turned blue because it didn't have oxygen. But despite these stories, cats cannot steal the breath of a child.

In recent years, some people have tried to put a modern spin on the breath-sucking tale. They claimed that family cats grow jealous when a new baby is brought home. To deal with

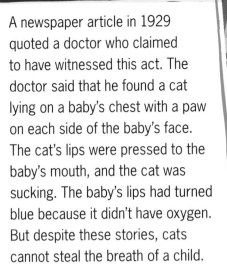

Some cats are curious about newborn babies.

the intruder, the jealous cat lies on top of the baby. It stays on top until it smothers the baby, and the baby stops breathing. However, while cats may be jealous, they cannot plot a baby's murder. They sometimes ignore a new baby, or they may hide from it.

How did this story get its start? No one knows for sure. But it's possible that cats were blamed when a baby died in its sleep of unknown causes. When people didn't have an explanation for a baby's death, they chose to blame cats.

Do Camels Really Store Water in Their Humps?

NO! A camel's hump does not hold water. Instead, the hump stores fat. When camels do not have enough food, they use the fat in their humps for nourishment.

A camel can live without food for two weeks. That is important for camels because they live in the desert, where food is often hard to find. When food is scarce, a camel digests the fat stored in its hump. The hump shrinks and becomes limp and flabby.

The camel on the left has humps that are limp.

Usually camels eat thorny plants, dry grasses, and desert bushes. But a hungry camel will eat almost anything. It will chew on people's tents, sandals, ropes, and blankets.

In the winter, camels do not need to drink. They get enough water from the scrubby plants that they eat. Camels can also trek under the summer sun for several days without water. When you get hot, you lose water by sweating. Sweat helps keep your body cool. Camels conserve water by letting their body temperature rise instead of sweating. A camel's temperature can swing from 93 to 107°F (34 to 42°C).

You can tell how healthy a camel is by looking at its hump. Well-fed camels have humps that stand up straight. The hump can weigh 80 pounds (36 kilograms).

Even with their swinging temperatures, camels lose lots of water in the desert heat. They can lose 30 percent of the water in their bodies and still be fine. When water is available, camels drink and drink until they have replaced the lost water. A camel can drink 30 gallons (114 liters) of water in ten minutes.

This camel is a dromedary camel, with one hump. The camel on page 36 is a Bactrian camel, with two humps.

One Hump or Two?

There are two different types of camels: dromedary camels and Bactrian camels. A dromedary camel has one hump on its back. Bactrian camels have two.

GLOSSARY

blood-brain barrier: a special layer of cells that prevents diseases and most parasites from entering the brain

echolocation: a method for locating an object by directing sounds toward it and listening to the echoes that bounce off

fledgling: a young bird that has grown feathers and is learning to fly

gills: organs that fish use to breathe

gizzard: a thick-walled pouch in the stomachs of some birds. Birds use their gizzards to grind food.

hibernate: to go into a sleeplike state during the winter

Kevlar: a material used to make bulletproof vests

migrate: to move from one region to another

nestling: a baby bird that is not ready to be out of the nest

nocturnal: active at night

nutrients: vitamins and minerals in food

olfactory lobe: the part of the brain that detects odors

parasite: a living thing that lives on another living thing, called a host. A parasite does not contribute to its host's survival.

pheromone: a chemical substance that is released by an animal and that causes a response in another animal of the same species

population: all the people or animals of a particular type that are living in a specified area

predator: an animal that hunts and eats other animals

prehensile: adapted for wrapping around an object. An opossum's tail is prehensile.

protein: a chemical that is part of living cells and is necessary for growth and repair in living organisms

SELECTED BIBLIOGRAPHY

"All About Birds: Orphaned Birds." Cornell Lab of Ornithology. 2007. http://www.birds.cornell.edu/AllAboutBirds/attracting/challenges/orphaned (January 15, 2008).

Florida Museum of Natural History. "Shark Attacks in Perspective," Ichthyology at the Florida Museum of Natural History. 1991. http://www.flmnh.ufl.edu/fish/sharks/Attacks/perspect.htm (January 19, 2008).

Kruszelnicki, Karl. "Great Moments in Science: Lemming Suicide Myth." ABC Science. April 7, 2004. Available online at http://www.abc.net.au/science/k2/moments/s1081903.htm (February 16, 2008).

Manzo, Andrea. "Brain Worms and Brain Amoebas: They Do Exist." *Engineering and Science* 66, 4 (2003). Available online at http://eands.caltech.edu/articles/LXVI4/brainworms.html (February 20, 2008).

Reuters. "You Can Teach an Old Dog New Tricks—with the Right Diet." *Science-Daily* 27 (September 2007). http://www.sciencedaily.com/releases/2007/09/070923202538.htm (January 20, 2008).

Smithsonian, "Bat Facts." Encyclopedia Smithsonian. N.d. http://www.si.edu/Encyclopedia_SI/nmnh/batfacts.htm (January 19, 2008).

FURTHER READING

Animal Myths, *MythBusters*: Myth or Fact
http://dsc.discovery.com/fansites/
mythbusters/quiz/animals/animals.html
Decide whether eight common beliefs
about animals are true or false in this
quiz from *MythBusters*—the popular
Discovery Channel television show.

Animal Myths Busted
http://kids.nationalgeographic.com/
Stories/AnimalsNature/Animal-myths
-busted
Read about different animal myths and
find out why they're false.

Berger, Melvin. *Can Snakes Crawl
Backward? Questions and Answers about
Reptiles.* New York: Scholastic, 2001.
Learn amazing facts about snakes,
lizards, alligators, and crocodiles.

Bruchac, Joseph. *Native American Stories.*
Myths and Legends series. Golden, CO:
Fulcrum Publishing, 1991. Read twenty-
four stories about animals, which show
their importance to Native Americans.

Crisp, Marty. *Everything Dog: What Kids
Really Want to Know about Dogs.*
Chanhassen, MN: NorthWord Press,
2003. Find the answers to thirty
questions about dogs.

Donovan, Sandy. *Does an Apple a Day
Keep the Doctor Away? And Other
Questions about Your Health and
Body.* Minneapolis: Lerner Publications
Company, 2010. Read true answers to
interesting questions in this book about
health and the human body.

Ganeri, Anita. *I Wonder Why Camels Have
Humps and Other Questions about
Animals.* Boston: Kingfisher, 2003. Find
out the difference between sharks and
dolphins, frogs and toads, monkeys and
apes, and other animals.

Llewellyn, Claire. *The Best Book of Sharks.*
Boston: Kingfisher, 1999. Discover
where sharks live, how they survive, and
the problems they face.

INDEX

ACKNOWLEDGMENTS
The images in this book are used with the permission of:
© Flirt/SuperStock, pp. 1, 5 (background), 11;
© Gerry Bishop/Visuals Unlimited, Inc., pp. 2 (top), 5;
© Cusp/SuperStock, pp. 2 (bottom), 14-15; © Ronald
Wittek/dpa/CORBIS, pp. 3 (top), 23 (bottom); © Hemis.fr/
SuperStock, pp. 3 (bottom), 37 (bottom); © Kim Taylor/
Dorling Kindersley/Getty Images, p. 4; © Gerry Lemmo,
pp. 6, 7 (top), 18, 20, 21 (top), 25 (bottom), 29, 32, 33;
© Steve Vidler/SuperStock, p. 7 (bottom); © Pacific Stock/
SuperStock, p. 8; © David Fleetham/Photographer's
Choice/Getty Images, p. 9 (top); © Brian Skerry/National
Geographic/Getty Images, p. 9 (middle); © SuperStock/
SuperStock, p. 9 (bottom); © Steve Cole/Photodisc/Getty
Images, pp. 10-11; © Mauritius/SuperStock, p. 12; © D&J
Bartlett/OSF/Animals Animals, p. 13 (top); © age fotostock/
SuperStock, pp. 13 (bottom), 16, 21 (bottom), 36; © David
Joel/Stone/Getty Images, p. 14; © ABW Photography/Super-
Stock, p. 15; © John Downer/Taxi/Getty Images, pp. 16-17;
© Jack Milchanowski/Visuals Unlimited, Inc., p. 17; © Dwight
Kuhn, p. 19; © Steve Maslowski/Visuals Unlimited, Inc.,
p. 22; © Zigmund Leszcynski/Animals Animals, p. 23 (top);
© Gay Bumgarner/Photographer's Choice/Getty Images,
p. 24; © Nigel Cattlin/Visuals Unlimited, Inc., p. 25 (top);
© Inga Spence/Visuals Unlimited, Inc., pp. 26-27; © Dean
Fox/SuperStock, p. 27; © Yoshio Otsuka/Amana Images/
Getty Images, pp. 28-29; © James Robinson/Animals
Animals, pp. 30-31; © Biosphoto/Gautier Christian/Peter
Arnold, Inc., p. 30; © RedChopsticks/Getty Images, p. 31;
© Erik Snyder/Stone/Getty Images, pp. 34-35; © Victoria
Peñafiel/Getty Images, p. 35; © Gertrud & Helmut Denzau/
naturepl.com, p. 37 (top).

Front Cover: © Nikki O'Keefe Images/Flickr/Getty Images.

Lerner Publications Company
A division of Lerner Publishing Group, Inc.
241 First Avenue North
Minneapolis, MN 55401 U.S.A.

Website address: www.lernerbooks.com

Library of Congress Cataloging-in-Publication Data

Silverman, Buffy.
    Can an old dog learn new tricks? : and other questions
about animals / by Buffy Silverman.
        p.   cm. — (Is that a fact?)
    Includes bibliographical references and index.
    ISBN 978–0–8225–9083–5 (lib. bdg. : alk. paper)
    1. Animals—Miscellanea— Juvenile literature. I. Title.
QL49.S5167 2010
590—dc22   2009020587

Manufactured in the United States of America
1 – JR – 12/15/09